AFFIRMING

John Gaskell

MAKING A RULE OF LIFE

Series Editor: Jeffrey John

DARTON · LONGMAN + TODD

First published in 1999 by
Darton, Longman and Todd Ltd
1 Spencer Court
140–142 Wandsworth High Street
London SW18 4JJ

in association with

Affirming Catholicism
St Luke's Centre
90 Central Street
London EC1V 8AQ

© 1999 John Gaskell

ISBN 0-232-52310-X

The views expressed in this book are those of the author and do not necessarily reflect any policy of Affirming Catholicism.

Designed and produced by Sandie Boccacci
in QuarkXPress on an Apple PowerMac
Set in 10/12½pt Times
Printed and bound in Great Britain by Page Brothers, Norwich

Affirming Catholicism

Affirming Catholicism is a movement (not an ecclesiastical party) which exists to do two things. We affirm our confidence in our Anglican heritage; and we seek to renew and promote the Catholic tradition within it. Our aim is to explore, explain and share with others both inside and outside the Church a lively, intelligent and inclusive Catholic faith. In the words of our Trust Deed:

> It is the conviction of many that a respect for scholarship and free enquiry has been characteristic of the Church of England and of the Churches of the wider Anglican Communion from earliest times, and is fully consistent with the status of those Churches as part of the Holy Catholic Church. It is desired to establish a charitable educational foundation which will be true both to those characteristics and to the Catholic tradition within Anglicanism ... The object of the foundation shall be the advancement of education in the doctrines and the historical development of the Church of England and the Churches of the wider Anglican Communion, as held by those standing within the Catholic tradition.

Our Publications

These are offered as one means of presenting Anglican Catholic teaching and practice in as clear and accessible a form as possible. Some cover traditional doctrinal and liturgical themes: others attempt to present a well-argued Catholic viewpoint on issues of debate currently facing the Church. There is a list of our series of booklets on page v.

The present series of books is provided, where appropriate,

with summaries to sections and suggested questions which we hope will facilitate personal study or discussion in groups. Other most recent titles in the series are:

Anglican Orders and the Priesting of Women Paul Avis
Introducing Richard Hooker and The Laws of Ecclesiastical Polity Martyn Percy
The Practice of Abortion: A Critique Michael Banner

To order these publications individually or on subscription, or for further information about the aims and activities of Affirming Catholicism, write to:

The Secretary
Affirming Catholicism
St Luke's Centre
90 Central Street
London EC1V 8AQ

Tel: 0171 253 1138
Fax: 0171 253 1139

Books in the Affirming Catholicism series

Affirming Confession John Davies
By What Authority? – Authority, Ministry and the Catholic Church Mark D. Chapman
Catholic Evangelism Stephen Cottrell
Catholicism and Folk Religion Jeremy Morris
Christian Feminism – An Introduction Helen Stanton
Christ in Ten Thousand Places – A Catholic Perspective on Christian Encounter with Other Faiths Michael Ipgrave
History, Tradition and Change – Church History and the Development of Doctrine Peter Hinchliffe
Humanity and Healing – Ministering to the Sick in the Catholic Tradition Martin Dudley
Imagining Jesus – An Introduction to the Incarnation Lewis Ayres
Is The Anglican Church Catholic? – The Catholicity of Anglicanism Vincent Strudwick
Is There an Anglican Way? – Scripture, Church and Reason: New Approaches to an Old Triad Ross Thompson
Lay Presidency at the Eucharist Benedict Green
'Making Present' – The Practice of Catholic Life and Liturgy Christopher Irvine
Marriage, Divorce and the Church Anthony E. Harvey
The Ministry of Deliverance Dominic Walker OGS
'Permanent, Faithful, Stable' – Christian Same-Sex Partnerships Jeffrey John
Politics and the Faith Today – Catholic Social Vision for the 1990s Kenneth Leech
Trinity and Unity Jane Williams
What is Affirming Catholicism? Jeffrey John
Why Women Priests? – The Ordination of Women and the Apostolic Ministry Jonathan Sedgwick

About the Author

In 1990 John Gaskell hosted the first meeting of Affirming Catholicism at the Church of Saint Alban the Martyr, Holborn. As priest there, his parish in the London Borough of Camden included Leather Lane Market, a modern Church school and the thriving St Alban's Centre. Now retired, he is an honorary Assistant Priest at All Saints', Margaret Street, in London's West End.

Contents

Introduction

> The Catholic tradition challenges us to structure the whole of our lives with Christ as the centre. It encourages us to make a rule of life, a pattern of worship each Sunday and feast day, with personal prayer and Bible reading. Spiritual direction and regular sacramental confession are opportunities to open ourselves to God.

This book is a response to that Affirming Catholicism affirmation and hopes to help the reader to draw up a Rule of Life. To be a Christian is not of course a matter of successful obedience to rules; it is living a Christ-centred life. That centring on our Lord, however, is promoted and prompted by having clear intentions of what we propose to do about participation in the life of the Church which is his Body.

The chapters which follow suggest what requires decision. After reflection upon them the reader should draw up a written Rule which applies to his or her circumstances as they now are and offer it to God in his Son's name. As time passes it can be revised, but for the present it will be a help in living the Catholic life, forming your spirituality by regular habits.

You will know that some people 'always go to mass on Tuesday evenings' or 'make a point of going to the annual Quiet Day'. There are many means of grace other than those touched on in this booklet and you may well want to make a rule about some of them. The questions considered here are commitment to public worship, private prayer, Bible reading and study, the Sacrament of Reconciliation or Confession, and giving. Finally we reflect on the benefits of guidance in the Way.

Worship

'Thank God it's Sunday', John Betjeman used to declare. He relished the day, and it would have been hard to imagine him not 'in church'. But there are lots of other things to do, and therefore the first item in one's Rule of Life will be Sunday worship. Living the Christian life is not a purely private matter nor a challenge to individual spiritual and moral achievement, but an experience of God's love and purpose for his creatures in which we engage with our fellow men, women and children. Its supreme expression is the Sunday mass, so we need a rule about it.

Because the Sacrament of Holy Communion is a means of grace, the Sunday Eucharist brings us strength from Jesus Christ for living our lives as his followers. With its readings from Holy Scripture, its address which is a preaching of the Word of God, its general prayer for the living and the dead and its great thanksgiving prayer in which the Church proclaims to God the eternal sacrifice of Jesus's life, death and resurrection, it sums up the patterns and purposes of Christian life. It is completed by Holy Communion, in which priest and people share sacramentally in the Body and Blood of Our Lord. This is why we say that the mass matters.

It is rooted in the earliest Christian days. Here is the way Saint Justin the Martyr recounts the practice of his time. He came from Palestine, taught in Rome, and died there, being beheaded for his faith in about 165 AD.

> On the day which is called Sun-day, all, whether they live in the town or the country, gather in the same place.
>
> Then the memoirs of the Apostles, or the Writings of the Prophets are read for as long as time allows.
>
> When the reader has finished, the president speaks, exhorting us to live by these noble teachings.
>
> Then we rise together and pray.
>
> Then as we said earlier, when the prayer is finished, bread, wine and water are brought. The president then prays and gives thanks as well as he can. And all the people reply with the acclamation, 'Amen'.
>
> Then the eucharistic gifts are distributed and shared out to everyone, and the deacons are sent to take them to those who are absent.

You notice that the Christians are recorded as 'gathering'. In doing so they are following a pattern which had already emerged in the days when the various books of the New Testament were being written. The early Christian community at Jerusalem is thus described in Acts 2:42 and 46:

> These remained faithful to the teaching of the Apostles, to the brotherhood, to the breaking of bread and to the prayers. . . . They went as a body to the Temple every day but met in their houses for the breaking of bread.

In the account in Acts 20 of a visit by St Paul to Troas, a town on the west coast of Turkey, the narrator writes: 'On the first day of the week we met to break bread' (v. 7). This was the dreadful occasion when young Eutychus was overcome by sleep during Paul's sermon and fell out of the window! These are evidences of the new Christian community's emerging recognition that the bread-breaking sealed and signified their fellowship with each other, with Our Lord Jesus Christ and God himself. The Holy Spirit made the bread over which they offered thanks to God the sacramental Body of their Lord; and in the power of the same Holy Spirit, and strengthened by that sacrament, they went out to be the Body of Christ in the world. They discovered in their communal worship a continuing expression of the experience of Jesus and the Twelve in the upper room before his trial and execution.

St Paul and St Luke were clear that this was what Jesus had intended. In writing to the Church at Corinth in southern Greece – as recorded in 1 Corinthians 11:23–7 – Paul describes the tradition he knows, and reminds them that Jesus instructed his friends to 'do this as a memorial of me'. There was a command of continuance and communion that came from the Christ himself.

> This is what I received from the Lord, and in turn passed on to you: that on the same night that he was betrayed, the Lord Jesus took some bread, and thanked God for it and broke it, and he said, 'This is my body, which is for you; do this as a memorial of me'. In the same way he took the cup after supper, and said, 'This cup is the new covenant in my blood. Whenever you drink it, do this as a memorial of me.' Until the Lord comes, therefore, every time you eat this bread and drink this cup, you are proclaiming his death, and so anyone who eats the bread or drinks the cup of the Lord unworthily will be behaving unworthily towards the body and blood of the Lord.

Luke's account of the matter is as follows:

> He took some bread, and when he had given thanks, broke it and gave it to them, saying, 'This is my body which will be given for you; do this as a memorial of me'. He did the same with the cup after supper, and said, 'This cup is the new covenant in my blood which will be poured out for you.' (22:19-20)

The regular obedience to this command soon became centred upon the first day of the week as a regular commemoration of the Lord's resurrection. Eventually as the missionary faith moved away from Jerusalem, Christian attendance at the Jerusalem Temple became a thing of the past – in any case it was Temple intrigue that in the providence of God had brought Jesus to his death.

Our Lord's sacrificial dying and rising replaced the cultus offered there to God, and Temple worship came to an end with its destruction by the Roman army in 70 AD. At the same time, the Christian communities recognised their own authentic life in the Holy Spirit, and their Jewish members gave up their attendance at the synagogue, the Jewish religious meetings. New Christians were less and less likely to be Jewish anyway. But they found in their Christian assemblies the power and the presence of their dead and resurrected Lord.

Jewish revelation had consecrated the seventh day of the week to the worship of God. No event less cataclysmic than the rising of Jesus from the tomb could suffice to change that law. Changed it was. Here is Paul writing to the Corinth Church around AD 57.

> Now about the collection made for the saints [i.e. church members in Jerusalem]: you are to do as I told the Churches in Galatia to do. Upon the first day of the

> week each one of you must put aside what he can afford, so that collections need not be made after I have come. (1 Corinthians 16:1-2)

Thus hundreds of years later my mother was always careful to have ready a silver threepenny bit inside her glove as she went to cathedral evensong on Sunday!

Our first predecessors in the faith lived in a world of religion and religions. Our own Christianity as we seek to live it out as Catholics in the Anglican Church is a choice against the general indifference of the day as well as a multiplicity of other religious options. To commit yourself to attending the Lord's service on the Lord's Day by a rule shows where you stand. There is perhaps for us no authority to tell us that we are obliged to go to mass because we are Christians. But as all Sundays celebrate the paschal mystery of the death and resurrection of the Lord, we will recognise an imperative from the Church to play our part. A rule encourages us in doing so.

To have made a rule is to settle in our minds and wills what our duty to God and his Church requires. We do not go to mass simply to benefit from it, or to watch reverently what others do, but to be a part of the active, worshipping, priestly people. If one is not there the witness of the Church to God, to its own members and to the world is impoverished. Absence is the loss of an expansive and encouraging experience of the Holy for oneself, and also a diminishment for the others. Living the life of grace demands using the means of grace for thanksgiving and renewal. Jesus himself comes to us as we receive his sacrament.

Your rule might say, 'I will attend the Saint So-and-So's 10.30 Parish Eucharist every week' or it might say, 'I will go to mass every Sunday', recognising that different circumstances might suggest an 'early service' before going out for the day or finding a church elsewhere when away for work or holiday.

The commitment that this invites – although it has been the universal rule of Christians for centuries – has special challenges today. What do you do about mass if you or the family or your close friends want to spend a morning in the local shopping mall – because shopping is a way of entertainment today and can almost be a way of life? John Betjeman wrote sadly of 'lonely shopping in a brilliant arcade', but he would find escalators and a crowd about him now. What course are you to pursue if all the expectations are that Sunday is an opportunity for time-consuming leisure activities – Thorpe Park, Alton Towers, cricket? What of the family duties such as ferrying offspring to sports training or distant friends? There are other expectations of travel, too, not least for business. While many have no employment, for others work is a time-consuming commitment, sometimes with very varied working hours. Thus it is hardly possible for a Christian man or woman to avoid the occasional conflict between employment and Christian obligation.

After reflection, therefore, your rule should include some plan of how you intend to make alternative arrangements, such as to go to mass on a Saturday evening – if that is an available provision – or in the week.

We have been reflecting on a worship rule as an individual might begin to formulate it. No rule, however, can expect to work unless it is in loving, realistic touch with the needs of others in a marriage or a family or a relationship of some other kind.

A Christian couple should have a rule for their Christian worship so that receiving Holy Communion together is part of the joy of being together at the weekend. The needs of children of various ages must be considered, as also the different expectations or prejudices of a spouse or partner. One of the tests which the worship rule will undergo will be the inevitable occasional conflicts of loyalties and interests.

Participation in eucharistic worship on Sunday is, then, a priority. But there are other days in the year, great feasts and other days of commemoration, which the Church has come to regard as having similar importance, and which we are also encouraged to observe by attendance at mass.

In addition to the great festivals which are observed on a Sunday – Easter, Pentecost or Whitsun, and Trinity Sunday – the principal feasts which are observed are Christmas Day, the Epiphany (6 January), the Presentation of Christ in the Temple (2 February or alternatively the Sunday between 28 January and 3 February), the Annunciation of Our Lord to the Blessed Virgin Mary, also called Lady Day (25 March), Ascension Day and All Saints' Day (1 November or the Sunday between 30 October and 5 November). These are days for attending mass and receiving Holy Communion if possible. Ash Wednesday, Maundy Thursday and Good Friday are principal holy days. Other days you might wish to observe are the festival for the Blessed Virgin Mary on 15 August and All Souls' Day on 2 November.

Making a rule about the Eucharist is an invaluable framework for our Christian life and growth. But of course it is not the end of the world if we do not always manage to keep it. The value of the rule is that we can return to it when we have lapsed from it!

> Let us keep firm in the hope we profess, because the one who made the promise is faithful. Let us be concerned for each other, to stir a response in love and good works. Do not stay away from the meetings of the community, as some do, but encourage each other to go. (Hebrews 10:23-5)

Heb 10. 23-25

This loving invitation still speaks to us today.

Private Prayer

The first duty and love for a Catholic Christian is the worship of God – Father, Son and Holy Spirit. Its sum and its source in the earthly life of the Church is the Sunday Eucharist or mass – also called the Liturgy or Holy Communion – and in it the faithful begin the new week after six other days in which prayer and worship will have had their part. One item in a Christian's Rule of Life, therefore, will be the planning of a definite programme for praying during the week, with perhaps both daily and weekly patterns.

Everyone needs his or her quiet time with God, recognising that we pray through Jesus Christ Our Lord and in the power of the Holy Spirit. The saints past and present and the angels too provide the circumstances of our prayer as do the challenges, hopes and failures of our own lives and personalities. This chapter looks at the various parts which constitute verbal prayer; but no analysis is of much use without a decision – after reflection – on when and where one is going to pray.

Bedtime – with its opportunity for thankfulness for the day and review of how we have served our Lord in our dealings – suits some people very well. In coming to a conclusion about that time of day, however, we have to think of family habits: do we, perhaps, need to take a spouse or children or invalids into consideration? There is also the question of whether the last minutes of our waking are appropriate for a serious endeavour in prayer?

Simply seeking to rest in the Lord might well be enough at the very end of the day: the main prayer time might come earlier. Again, for a busy teenager or student, with so much to do, last thing at night might seem to be the only possibility!

Serious commitment might mean the choice of some time when getting up in the morning. Anyone might offer an act of praise on waking, with the sign of the cross, the Lord's Prayer, the Hail Mary and the 'Glory be to the Father . . .', but to have some fuller time to himself or herself at the very beginning of the day for some will be the best plan. For others it might be after the children have gone off to school, or in a local church during the lunch-break, or before doing the dinner. Think realistically of what your opportunities are and decide accordingly. On Friday or Saturday we need to begin to look forward to attending mass and receiving Holy Communion on the Lord's Day. If you 'simply must' see a particular soap or you 'always go to Bingo on Saturday night', in the same way you can make it a duty and a matter of thought to decide how you 'simply must' make some preparation for Sunday. This booklet cannot tell you what to decide – but it does invite your decision.

To be a Catholic Christian is to be a man or woman or child who prays – that is, seeks time to raise the mind and the heart to God. We need to think about the parts of prayer so that we can consider how our prayer-life is shaping and what we might do to improve it.

Here are two vivid accounts of prayer: they come from Donald Nicholl's *Triumphs of the Spirit in Russia* (published by Darton, Longman & Todd, 1997).

Donald Nicholl

It is true, of course, as some critics are fond of repeating, that Tolstoy did not copy down word for word the stories that were current among the lowly people but shaped the stories for a wider audience. Nevertheless we know that Tolstoy was for ever talking with pilgrims and peasants and listening to them in inns and monasteries, on the road and at his home. He is among the most reliable of witnesses to that by which the people lived – more reliable, certainly, than critics a hundred years later who have never made a pilgrimage on foot or spoken with peasants.

One person, for instance, from whose lips Tolstoy heard his tale was the peasant story-teller, Vasily Petrovich Shchegolynok. Tolstoy met him in 1879 or 1880 and, in his irrepressibly direct manner, asked Shchegolynok how he prayed. Whereupon Shchegolynok spontaneously poured forth a prayer of epic proportions in the course of which he called upon innumerable saints and martyrs. Tolstoy was deeply moved, and after bidding Shchegolynok goodbye he turned to his aristocratic companion with the words: 'That is how to pray, not as how the likes of you and I do.'

I think that Tolstoy did not notice that the pray-er was a professional story-teller, a man of words, used to pouring them forth.

The second account is an episode in Tolstoy's *War and Peace*. Pierre and Platon are prisoners who have just recently *not* been shot for setting Moscow on fire. It is late at night. Eventually Platon says,

'Well, I think you must be sleepy', and begins crossing

himself rapidly and constantly repeating: 'Lord Jesus Christ, holy Saint Nicholas, Frola and Lavra! Lord Jesus Christ, have mercy on us and save us', he concluded; then bowed to the ground, got up, sighed, and sat down again on his heap of straw. 'That's the way. Lay me down like a stone, O God, and raise me up like a loaf', he muttered as he lay down, pulling his coat over him.

'What prayer was that you were saying?' asked Pierre.

'Eh?' murmured Platon, who had almost fallen asleep, 'what was I saying? I was praying. Don't you pray?'

'Yes, I do', said Pierre. 'But what was that you said: Frola and Lavra?'

'Well, of course', replied Platon quickly, 'the horses' saints. One must pity the animals too. Eh, the rascal! Now you've curled up and got warm, you daughter of a bitch!' said Karataev, touching the dog that lay at his feet. And again turning over he fell asleep immediately.

For a long time Pierre did not sleep, but lay with eyes open in the darkness listening to the regular snoring of Platon, who lay beside him, and he felt that the world that had been shattered was once more stirring in his soul with a new beauty and on new and unshakeable foundations.

Both these stories are of faithful and sincere prayer in the Russian tradition. The Western Catholic – Roman or Anglican – engages also in a living tradition of verbal prayer – that is, prayer using words – that embodies the Christian's expression of faith, hope and love towards God.

There are recognisable parts to prayer: adoration; confession; thanksgiving; intercession and petition. Sometimes they are put over as a little mnemonic of ACTS – Adoration, Confession, Thanksgiving and Supplication. These are the four elements of praying, which can be used as a pattern. For a decade in my late twenties when I said my prayers, that was the pattern I followed at the end of the day: adoration came first, then some prayers of confession, thanksgiving, intercession and petition. (I knew that something had happened when the subject of ordination moved from petition to thanksgiving!)

Adoration

Adoration is first: that is the Lord's pattern. God is addressed simply for being himself, as himself, first in importance and first in order. All our prayer goes to God who has revealed himself as the Son and Holy Spirit. Here at once we are confronting the mystery and wonder of our faith: the Almighty and Everlasting God invites us to address him as Father, just as Jesus did. We perhaps address Jesus and he, as our great High Priest, offers our prayer. We call upon the intercession of Our Lady, or Saint Nicholas or, like Platon, the horses' saints and they pass our prayer on. The great stream of prayer as it ascends from the world and through the Church goes to God the Holy Trinity.

Concern with God comes first in the pattern of the Lord's own Prayer, Jesus's model instructions to his disciples. In St Matthew's Gospel, it is in the Sermon on the Mount:

> 'Our Father in heaven,

may your name be held holy,
your kingdom come,
your will be done,
on earth as in heaven.' (6:9-10)

In St Luke's Gospel it is recorded in a different situation: Jesus has been away praying by himself and when he returns to join his friends they ask him to instruct them in prayer, so that they may do what he does. St Luke's Lord's Prayer is very brief at this point: 'Father, may your name be held holy, your kingdom come' (Luke 11:2). It is difficult really to decide which of those two versions gives us the authentic voice of Jesus. The important thing is that Jesus puts our heavenly Father first and he invites us to address God as 'Father', even though he is our Creator and our Lord. Thus we find ourselves raised to the height to which all prayer is to go.

Perhaps when we begin to pray to the all-holy Father we shall need first to stir up our sense of the holy. We kneel. We make the sign of the cross, the symbol of God's love. We say: 'In the name of the Father and of the Son and of the Holy Spirit.' We place before us that pattern of what God is like. Maybe we turn briefly over in our minds the implications of the word 'Father', that he has sent the Son to be the salvation of the world and through him to make the Church by the giving of the Holy Spirit. Many people will be moved in their adoration of God by the wonders and majesty of the natural world, even by the achievements of humankind. We turn to the Maker inspired by what we see in his making. As often as not, however, our adoration of God will flow from our love of Our Lord Jesus Christ. St John puts into the mouth of

Jesus these words: 'To have seen me is to have seen the Father' (John 14:9) and much of our adoring prayer to God will come from our understanding and worship of Jesus. That is why a crucifix has so much to tell us when we come to the time of prayer.

When I was twenty-one my Uncle Archibald gave me twenty-one shillings – a guinea – as a present. I spent it on a crucifix at Mowbray's Bookshop in Margaret Street in London, knowing that my parents could never object because it was 'Arch's present' but would have greatly disapproved if I had simply bought it as a churchy whim. It hangs in the room where I write now. When mind or heart can find no words of prayer it is enough simply to stand before it. It is a present with presence! The image of the crucified Lord also helps one to raise heart and mind to God when words do come and Catholics for centuries have found in it stimulus for prayer and encouragement for life.

Confession

It needs to be said also before embarking on 'C for Confession' that a very important meaning which can be attached to this letter 'C' is the notion of Contrition. 'C' stands not merely for acknowledging your sins – that is, confessing them – but being contrite about them – that is, reaching such a measure of sorrow as, by the Holy Spirit, you can.

Confession and thanksgiving very much belong to each other. This is very important because at any moment when we pray we are setting out on our pilgrimage towards our heavenly fulfilment and we start from where we are. We do not start as a different person: we do not start with some of our dreams or delusions. We start from where we are, with the things which are wrong about us and the things which are good about us. Yet clearly any man or woman who prays will have dreams and delusions. As we bring them to God in prayer and reflection they may identify themselves as realisable or regrettable or as harmless fantasy. Thus as we think about those aspects of ourselves we recognise that the whole person will seek to pray and prayer will lead to purification, or to praise.

Every day, therefore, there should be a brief examination of conscience – how have we served our Lord in thought, word and deed and in what we have failed to do or be? We are placed by God in his world to be responsible to him: as Providence has so far led us how have we done today? With the friendship of the Lord who shares himself with us at the altar and in the Church's varied life we need have no fear.

When you contemplate 'C' for Contrition and 'C' for Confession do not be downcast. Contrition is not being gloomy. Being sorry about our sins is not a form of inward-looking glumness. We look at our sins and we recognise that in God's love they are false ways of being ourselves of which God has much to make! We cannot start from anywhere else but where we are now. And Christ is with us in the whole circumstances of our life. How very hard praying can be if we are trying to embark on honesty with God. It leads to honesty with ourselves. Thus we come before him with sorrow for our shortcomings and thankfulness for our virtues, our gifts and our graces.

As we pray, we are in the presence of God's Majesty, but because he is love and there is no other God than the

God who has been revealed in the teaching and the passion and the death and the resurrection of Jesus and the giving of the Spirit to make the Church, we are safe and free to acknowledge our sins to ourselves and to him. Perhaps we shall recognise as the Spirit moves us to contrition that we ought to confess our sins. Thus every examination of conscience and prayer of confession looks forward to the next opportunity, whenever it may be, of making our confession to the Church in the person of God's priest. Further, just as every thanksgiving looks forward to the great thanksgiving of the next Eucharist which we are to attend, so every prayer of confession also looks forward to our participation in the liturgical general confession at mass.

In contrition and confession we are not trying to work up any false guilt or to develop in ourselves a false sense of our weakness. We can, however, usefully recognise that one of the tasks of the Christian man or woman is to be sorry for the sins of the world. As part of the priestly people, I come bearing my own sins but I also recognise in my common humanity that I also bear my part in being sorry for the sins that go on in the world, although I am not directly responsible. There should in a sense be something 'green' about all of us when we come to make our confession. We acknowledge the shortcomings of humanity in general in our use of the world and our use of each other. We ought to make 'politically correct' prayers of confession on behalf of the world. This is not to suggest that we should fall for that sort of 'we are all guilty' talk. As priestly people, rather, we come to make our confessions on the part of all.

Thanksgiving

The joyful subject of thanksgiving follows, for as priestly people we offer the world's thanks and praise.

Over and over again when you read the epistles of St Paul you find the wonderful tone of his voice raised in thankfulness to God: 'We always mention you in our prayers and give thanks for you all.' That is Paul and Silas and Timothy writing to the Thessalonians. It is delightful to see that thanksgiving comes right at the beginning of that Letter, as of seven of Paul's Letters, and is at the heart of a life lived in the gospel.

At every mass we remember how our Lord Jesus Christ gave thanks at the Last Supper. We remember the joy of our Lord Jesus Christ in what he was doing.

On Good Friday we remember the triumph of Jesus in saying: 'It is finished.' That sort of thankfulness for God's creation, flawed though it is, for humanity, sinful though we are, and for ourselves is something that should invest every Christian man and woman's prayer. The main trigger will always be – will it not? – the passion and the death and the resurrection of the Lord. That's why Platon in *War and Peace* was so right. At the beginning of his praying time he made the sign of the cross *over and over again*. When, perhaps, we are at a bit of a loss to know what to think, or say or feel, we can do very much worse than doing just the same ourselves. Going to our cross in our room, or making the cross on our body as the sign of the power of the love of God coming into the world, moves us to prayer. Thankfulness for the redemption of the world, 'for the means of grace and for the hope of glory' as the Prayer Book General Thanksgiving puts it, will provide the frame for our own thanksgivings and for people and events in the Church and the world.

Supplication

'S' is for Supplication which covers intercession and petition.

As I have been preparing this book I have been very much reminded of one of my sisters-in-law who – I suppose about thirty years ago – was involved in programmes on the TV about pre-natal care. It was a subject she knew about. During discussion of the series, because she knew the subject, she kept on saying, 'But we must mention so-and-so', or 'What about telling the mother-to-be this?', or 'What about that?' The producer of the series got rather fed up with her and said: 'You must remember, Mrs Gaskell, this is a TV programme; we can't bother with extraneous information.'

In a similar way, over and over again as you discuss prayer you realise that there are so many points that might be made. One preliminary of some importance is that prayer is a unity. We may talk about the parts of prayer one after the other in order of importance or in order of performance but they all link up. So at the moment when I am glorifying God my heart may move me into words of thanksgiving; as I am moving perhaps in the area of confession I shall be moved to petition; or as I think of the person I've offended, to intercession. Thus prayer in my own words may lead into quotations from the mass or the creeds or the hymn-book.

As we think about supplication, taking intercession first, we need to look again at the opening lines of the Lord's Prayer in Matthew and Luke, which we considered briefly at the beginning of the chapter. Neither of those prayers really gives us a prayer of intercession as we would understand it now. But it is, we note, a prayer in the plural. It is assumed that we pray as men and women in fellowship with others. In St Matthew's Gospel we pray 'Our Father' and while St Luke simply gives us the word 'Father', it is a prayer uttered by disciples together. It is helpful when we are thinking about praying for others, therefore, always to remember that it is a way of taking part in the Communion of Saints, that is, the fellowship of Christian men, women and children on earth now and glorified in heaven. Also we are acting as representatives, as the priestly people of God, for all humanity. The Communion of Saints is awaiting to be engulfed by all the populations, and as we pray for others that is the sort of background and destiny we need to have in mind.

While we can utter a general prayer for the world, we cannot of course pray 'in detail' for everybody! That is why it is important to have an intercession list, so that we can care for particular people and needs as representative of the whole yearning of the universe for the God whom we address. We need information if we can get it and – if we can apply it – imagination. Yet it is a mistake to think that our intercessory prayer needs very much detail. A public general intercession at mass illustrates this, and can sometimes be very moving. There we demonstrate the fact that intercession does not require that you know 'all about it'. We are asked to pray for 'Brenda', only perhaps a name, but momentarily we hold her in our minds and hearts and unite her through our prayer with the sacrificial offering of Our Lord Jesus Christ. Usually of course our charity demands embodiment and therefore it helps prayer to know of 'Rachel' perhaps that she has leukaemia, or of 'George' that he is in prison. That gives us something on which we can use our imagination as we attach our will and our intention of love for that person to offer him or her to God. God knows what they need: our task is to bring them to him.

It seems to be the pattern that God needs us men, women and children, so that his grace and goodness can be released into the world. At the time of intercession – whether we are on our feet praying for the Church and the world at church or on our knees at our bedside or desk – we are acting as the priestly people, his representatives in this world helping to achieve his purposes. To be a Christian is to be given the privilege of being called to be a channel of God's love. Often, of course, we are blocked channels, but nevertheless our vocation is there, greater and more momentous than we.

Some of us were astonished when Mrs Thatcher on the steps of Number Ten, having achieved electoral victory, uttered these words, but they are always worth pondering: 'Make me a channel of Your peace.' Using these or similar words, we bring our little love and feeble wills and make an offering of them in Christ Jesus on behalf of others.

Any Rule of Life therefore should include a list of persons for whom we intercede or causes which we ask God to guide and inspire, combined with clear intentions as to when we intend to pray. We might want to remember some sick friends frequently while they are ill. Causes such as the peace processes in Ulster or parts of the Middle East or Africa could be allotted a regular day. One could pray for the mission of the Church on Friday, the day of the cross, and perhaps on Sunday for the church of which one is a member. Dead friends and relatives should have their place, too.

Overwhelmed as we are by information, it might seem that it will be obvious what the needs are for which we should intercede at our prayer time. It is, however, a good idea to sort out in advance what the needs might be that provoke and interest us so that we may proceed to prayer at once when the time comes. Some of our intercessions of course must be based on a willed assessment of what love asks of us rather than on our individual feelings! Remember also that any list should be revised from time to time as Divine Providence moves things on.

This true story of faithfulness in intercession may encourage you. In 1935 a new vicar arrived in the London suburb in which my family lived. There had not been a church in the area before and the new parish priest did a lot of evangelistic and pastoral work by pursuing the many children in the district who had not been baptised. My parents did not want their children christened, but my mother went to see the priest to express both her convictions and her doubts. The priest was clear that the children should not be baptised just because he was pressing the idea, and the subject was dropped. He did, however, promise that he would pray for the two little boys. When I was ordained as a priest twenty-five years later, a friend of my parents mentioned it to the former vicar, now in a far-off parish. His quiet comment was: 'I have prayed for those two boys every month since I discussed them with their mother!' In the course of those many years of intercession 'the two little boys' had both been baptised in their teens and now one had been ordained.

Every exhortation to intercession or to confidence in

petition makes us wonder at the point of it all. Clearly many prayers are 'answered' in the sense that what we ask for is given – we ask that someone we love may be given strength in appalling sorrow or the virtue of fortitude in terrible illness and we observe their suffering survival and give thanks for it. The Christian may see here the loving work of God as Father and of Jesus Christ as healer. The sceptic may simply see a coincidence – but the ever faithful Archbishop Ramsey, when this was put to him, commented that he was thankful that sometimes when he prayed coincidences did seem to occur!

On the other hand, many prayers are *not* answered in the sense that what we ask for is given – famine still stalks the world; injustice and cynical political abuse do not abate; and as general war seems to decline we are still confronted by the utter cruelties of local violence. All these things fill the prayers of Christians and millions of others who pray. As we pray in union with the passion of the world, however, Christians will have before them the fact of Christ's cross and resurrection as the sign and guarantee of ultimate redemption. Such hopeless prayer is also for thousands the prompting to social action and political concern. Thus my prayers for the hungry may be 'answered' by a man deciding to do relief work or a woman making discoveries in a food-science laboratory, because to pray as a Catholic is to be embroiled in God's love for all.

So 'answer to prayer' is a less pressing concern as we grow in recognising the way in which our prayer life is a participation in the life of the Holy Trinity. God's own faith, hope and love find their expression through the phrases of faith, hope and love which we ourselves address to Father, Son and Holy Spirit or which we call upon Our Lady and the Saints to utter.

Turning now to petition we shall hear sophisticated people telling us that we should be able to do without it. Even as Christians we may sometimes feel that 'I should not presume to ask that'. For enlightenment here we go to the night-time of Jesus's prayer in the Garden of Gethsemane: 'Abba, Father, all things are possible to you: take this cup away from me' (Mark 14:36). That is the prayer you utter when you come away from the consultant and he has told you what is the matter with you. That is the prayer you utter when you are faced with the death of the beloved. That is the prayer you utter at all sorts of moments in life as you live out Christ's life. If Jesus was able to pray for release from the threat of tomorrow, we can rightly make our own requests. We believe that God is our loving Father. We recall that Jesus arose strengthened for what was to come.

Never forget that we do not pray alone. When we address Almighty God we do so 'in Christ', as part of his mystical Body the Church. We do it 'in the Spirit', scarcely to be distinguished from 'in Christ'. Our personalities are invested, though we resist it so much, with the Christ who is Our Lord and the Lord who is the Spirit. As members of the Catholic Church we belong to the Body of Christ and pray with the Saints supporting us as part of that Body in heaven.

We do of course suffer from much illusion – I ask, 'God, make me the Archbishop of Canterbury', or what might be rather nicer, 'the Patriarch of Venice'! We need to ask as fools so that we can find out what we should ask for. So my prayer may gradually conform to reality, God's will: 'God, you call me to be the Assistant Priest, Honorary, of All Saints', Margaret Street.' Thus there is a progression from asking God for what might well be right, and, as the Holy Spirit eliminates possibilities, we can actually move on until we are prepared for our final end.

Sometimes our petition for this or that will be inspired by the road-rage of life. We may need to utter that sort of prayer so that we can be healed of it. We find hope in our desperation and reconciliation in our disappointments, enlightenment in our blindness. All the time we are praying we are making ready for our final fulfilment, our end in glory and God.

Thus in looking at the four parts of prayer and the way in which they apply to the complex strands of our existence as we live it now, we recognise that they finally lead up to the Father, to be summed up in him.

Bible Reading

One of my oldest possessions is 'Grandma Davidson's Bible'. It is finely bound in dark brown leather with gold tooling, now worn with use and handling, and the title page is endorsed in splendid thick pencil handwriting 'Mrs Davidson, 20, Brailsford Road – Pew 13'. The print is small but clear, two columns to the page, with a third column of cross-references and literal translations. The book has no date, but Mrs Davidson perhaps owned it when she gave birth to my own grandma in 1861. The latter was at one time the only churchgoer I knew. When she died her daughter, my mother, passed the volume on to me. Now it stands neglected on the shelf. We can guess that by her it was in use regularly. Looking at it now, however, I find it hard to believe that at one time it was 'my Bible': no wonder I did not read it!

What should we do about Bible reading now? Just as our prayer at mass and our worshipping Sunday life leads on to the prayers of the week and the struggle and work of daily existence, so also the eucharistic readings prompt us to our own personal Bible reading. In the Holy Scriptures we have the foundation documents of the Catholic religion. They tell us about Our Lord Jesus Christ, put him in the historical context of the chosen people from whom he came and provide evidence about the immediate consequences of his life, death and resurrection and the giving of the Holy Spirit to make the Church. The analysis, study and exposition of these immensely varied documents composed and collated over a thousand years is the wonderful task of students and theologians. Their learning is one of the glories of the Church: their mediation to other Christians clearly and fruitfully is the task of our bishops, clergy and writers.

The Holy Scriptures are foundation documents in the history of salvation and its doctrinal understanding but they also make up most importantly *an inspired text which itself inspires*. We recognise it as containing the Word of God. We discover too that God's Word goes on being uttered to men, women and children as they read it now. Although, for example, the teaching stories of Jesus belong to another age and another culture from our own they are potent in communicating his message to us today. The circumstances in which some of the Old Testament prophets found God's inspiration to speak may be quite lost on us now without a commentator's guidance, but we can still hear the power and authority with which they spoke in Yahweh's name. We do not believe the myths at the beginning of Genesis as history but we see the sense of them. We doubt if Our Lord himself went round Palestine saying things like 'I am the light of the world' but we believe heartily that God's inspiration of St John's Gospel tells us the truth about his Son. The inspiration that went to produce these writings is re-evoked by our use of them today: they nourish our life and our thought as Church and as individuals.

As you are drawing up your Rule of Life, therefore, you should consider your commitment to reading the Bible. Its study is closely related to our prayer life because the events it describes, its picture language, its exposition of the significance of Our Lord Jesus Christ, all become part of our own thinking and shape our thoughts as we raise mind and heart to God. To make sure that our vision is a right one we keep in touch with the teaching of the Church through creed, sacrament and preaching, but we need to engage with the Scriptures ourselves so that our own personal vision may be clarified by God. Sometimes this must involve puzzling out what a passage means, because we have to avoid the error of giving our own meaning to it. As we read the Scriptures and hear the Word of God, we will, however, want to know 'What does it mean to me?'

How do I decide what parts of the Bible to read? One way to do that is to read 'with the Church'. The daily worship of the Church in Eucharist, Morning Prayer and Evening Prayer, has readings selected by authority. If you buy a lectionary such as *The New Lectionary and Calendar as authorised by the Church of England* you will find set out there all the details of the scriptural material required for the services. So for example at the Eucharist on 5 May 1998 Psalm 87 and readings from Acts and St John's Gospel were used; at Morning Prayer we read from Deuteronomy and Titus, and at Evening Prayer from Exodus and St Luke. On the next day, subsequent verses were read from each of these texts, and so the pattern continues. In using the lectionary for personal Bible reading you would choose each day to pursue just one of the lessons for the day, for example either from St John's Gospel, Deuteronomy or Titus. If you choose St John's Gospel for a period, when that is concluded you might transfer to one of the Old Testament readings. If you do not decide to pursue the pattern of a daily reading you can opt to read whatever is set out for the days you require.

BRF

The publications of the Bible Reading Fellowship* are a great help to Bible reading. *Guidelines* is a quarterly magazine – pocket sized – which provides suggestions for daily readings with commentaries about authorship, contents and meaning. For example, with the issue for January to April 1998, readers would have looked at parts of Exodus, Daniel, Mark and Isaiah together with all of 1 Corinthians and Jonah. In connection with the 1998 Lambeth Conference the BRF produced *Transforming Grace*, six weeks of daily readings and commentary on a study of 2 Corinthians. *New Daylight* includes daily Bible passages printed out in full with comment and prayer: available also in a large print edition. There is a special series of Bible readings for women called *Day by Day with God*. These pocket-sized booklets contain a few verses for each day, not always providing continuous reading from day to day, accompanied by comment and reflection, and could be a great help to a woman wanting a 'thought for the day' in a busy life.

When deciding on prayer times you might say that you will pray for ten minutes. With reading it is better probably to commit yourself to the passage set, pondering and praying as the Spirit prompts. As with other elements in your Rule of Life you should consider carefully what you can realistically intend regarding frequency and the time to settle down to read. The rule is not to be a target which you might hit at a much later stage of growth in the Faith but a setting out of what is reasonably to be expected now. This enables current achievements to be consolidated with

* Peter's Way, Sandy Lane West, Oxford OX4 5HG. (Tel: 01865 748227; Fax: 01865 773150)

the hope – and intention! – of moving on later. So if you consider your best plan is to have half an hour of Bible study on Friday night and not a daily, shorter time, put that down in the rule and ask God to strengthen you in it. That could perhaps mean for some a careful look at the mass readings for the Sunday following.

Bible reading is an essential work, for increasingly the great stories and themes of the Bible are not familiar to people. School daily assemblies may not include them, and R.I. is not compulsory for all. Not everyone goes to Sunday school or profits from it. We have an obligation as adults to the faith in which we live and work to renew ourselves in it by going back to the basics and making them again our own. Instructed by reason and tradition we wait upon God in and through his Scriptures.

Which Bible are we to read? For Grandma Davidson the only possible Bible was the Authorised Version. Known also as the King James' Version it has been joined since by revisions of it and by fresh translations of the original Hebrew and Greek writings. My own preferred Bible is The Jerusalem Bible with Short Introduction and Notes (1975) and the quotations from Holy Scripture in this booklet are taken from it. Very highly regarded is the New Revised Standard Version of the Bible. That was published in 1990, and in 1995 the Oxford University Press produced an Anglicized edition, considered both modern and majestic. The New English Bible which first appeared in 1961 is simpler and more direct. It is exhilarating that we live at a time in which fine work has been done in renewing the impact of the Holy Scriptures by fresh and distinguished translations. At the end of the second millennium we should use and treasure them as the

Authorised Version has been treasured in the past.

I wrote above that the foundations of Bible knowledge may or may not have been laid at school or Sunday school. When did we learn the outlines of the Faith? I certainly remember nothing about my confirmation classes except the rector's assertion, in replying to someone's question, that King Charles I was a Roman Catholic! Doubtless in my blank memory of early instruction I am not alone. Part of a Rule of Life I suggest, therefore, should be a commitment to study. One could promise to spend an hour a week reading, undertake membership of a parish study group or make a concerted effort to seek out informative TV programmes. Affirming Catholicism's booklets provide a little collection on which one could start, and the *News* and the *Journal** provide thoughtful articles and reviews of books which may attract. Perhaps as regards study a precise rule cannot be made but do have in your mind the hope and intention of it. Part of our witness as Catholic Christians will be to answer the occasional query that is put to us about the Faith and it must be our loving duty to make ourselves ready to answer.

* Affirming Catholicism, St Luke's Centre, 90 Central Street, London EC1V 8AQ. (Tel: 0171 253 1138; Fax: 0171 253 1139)

Reconciliation

Grant, we beseech you, merciful Lord,
to your faithful people pardon and peace,
that they may be cleansed from all their sins
and serve you with a quiet mind;
through Jesus Christ your Son our Lord,
who is alive and reigns with you,
in the unity of the Holy Spirit,
one God, now and for ever.
(Collect for the Twenty-first Sunday after Trinity)

A primary setting for thinking about reconciliation is provided at the end of St John's Gospel by the story of Jesus appearing to his disciples in the upper room.

In the evening of that same day, the first day of the week, the doors were closed in the room where the disciples were, for fear of the Jews. Jesus came and stood among them. He said to them, 'Peace be with you', and showed them his hands and his side. The disciples were filled with joy when they saw the Lord, and he said to them again, 'Peace be with you.'

'As the Father sent me,
so am I sending you.'

After saying this he breathed on them and said:

'Receive the Holy Spirit.
For those whose sins you forgive,

they are forgiven;
for those whose sins you retain,
they are retained.' (20:19-23)

It is the great reconciliation scene of the New Testament, when the group of disciples – not just the Twelve – are given pardon and peace. The resurrected Lord comes as a forgiver with a word of peace to settle their consciences. He evokes 'joy' to replace the joylessness of their betrayal and weakness. He has a gift of 'Spirit' for men and women who had no spirit left. We see in this story an embodiment of the Church as the writer of the fourth Gospel knew it. It is a Church dominated by the presence of the resurrected Lord, his hands and his feet and his side with the marks of the cross. But it is a Church founded on men and women who had fallen into fear, who had the doors locked for fear of their fellow Jews and had no spirit in them. The men and women in the upper room, unaware that the Lord was going to appear to them, represent us and help us to understand our life as Christians today. We find also in ourselves the joy and renewal which was theirs.

Every time we exchange the Peace at mass we act out an aspect of this resurrection appearance. As we say 'Peace be with you' we experience something of the joy that the disciples felt in the upper room. The Peace has been one of the great discoveries in the recent reforms of the liturgical life of Christians.

Christ's appearance in the upper room is also remembered at every ordination. The story is read as the eucharistic Gospel of the day, for the Church and its priests in every generation are a continuing sacrament of what John wrote about.

The former Secretary of the Church Pastoral Aid Society – not a notable Anglo-Catholic! – said these words as he laid his episcopal hands on my head:

> Receive the Holy Ghost for the office and work of a Priest in the Church of God, now committed unto thee by the imposition of our hands. Whose sins thou dost forgive, they are forgiven; and whose sins thou dost retain, they are retained. And be thou a faithful dispenser of the Word of God, and of His Holy Sacraments; in the name of the Father, and of the Son, and of the Holy Ghost. Amen.

All through the Middle Ages, and until recently in the Western Church of which we are a part, that is the prayer said by the bishop at the moment of ordaining a priest.

Amid the changes and chances of the Reformation era the Church of England and the other Anglican Churches have been quite clear about the absolving authority granted to a priest. The bishop's words quoted above come from the 1662 Ordinal attached to *The Book of Common Prayer*. The 1662 Prayer Book – which we should not use in the late twentieth century but should know what is in it – contains in the Visitation of the Sick the words that the priest is to utter when he absolves a penitent. (These words were also in the Prayer Books of 1549 and 1552.)

> Our Lord Jesus Christ, who hath left power to his Church to absolve all sinners who truly repent and believe in him, of his great mercy forgive thee thine offences: And by his authority committed to me, I

> absolve thee from all thy sins, In the name of the Father, and of the Son, and of the Holy Ghost. Amen.

The heart of the prayer is the declaration: 'I absolve thee.'

If we look again at the 1662 Prayer Book, we find, as part of the service for the celebration of the Holy Communion, a long Exhortation which was intended to be read occasionally by the parish priest before the Eucharist. This Exhortation invites the members of the congregation to come and 'open their grief', their private grief and need for pardon and peace. 'Come to the Vicar and make your confession', says the Exhortation, as a prompting to conscience.

> And because it is requisite, that no man should come to the Holy Communion, but with a full trust in God's mercy, and with a quiet conscience; therefore if there be any of you, who by this means cannot quiet his own conscience herein, but requireth further comfort or counsel, let him come to me, or to some other discreet and learned Minister of God's Word, and open his grief; that by the ministry of God's holy Word he may receive the benefit of absolution, together with ghostly counsel and advice, to the quieting of his conscience, and avoiding of all scruple and doubtfulness.

I mention these historical details because I think that it is very important to understand that going to confession as a sacramental sign is not just limited to Roman Catholics. Occasionally people are inclined to think that it's the sort of thing you do if you are devout but odd: 'It's really Roman Catholic.' Of course, it isn't 'really Roman Catholic' at all. All Orthodox Christians of every Rite go to confession. Numbers of penitents decline but in theory all Roman Catholics are obliged to seek 'pardon and peace' because of one of the decrees of the Lateran Council of 1215. The policy in the Church of England has largely been, since the Oxford Movement revived our use of this sacrament, that 'all may; none must; some should.' This view can suggest that you have either got to be wildly extravagant in sin or madly devout in devotion to go to confession. Yet in fact it should be part of the ordinary diet of all Christian men, women and children. It is part of God's generosity as his grace pours down into the universe of which he is Creator, and in which every one of us at some time or other needs 'pardon and peace'. It is not a High Church fad: it is part of the gospel.

Jesus said:

> 'Receive the Holy Spirit.
> For those whose sins you forgive,
> they are forgiven;
> for those whose sins you retain,
> they are retained.'

And, since that day, the bishops and priests of the universal Church have been offering pardon and peace from the risen Lord.

One of the reasons we all ought to go to confession, to be penitent and hear the words of absolution, is the need we all have to acknowledge the dark side of our life. One of the stresses of being a Christian is that sometimes we may feel that we are called upon to play a part – to be nice, or to attend things, or to subscribe – putting a face on it, one man or woman in their time playing many parts. And, alas, what a strain it is when we are trying to play several parts at once. Yet when I confess what I have said or thought or done wrong, or failed to do right, I am acknowledging the reality of an enormous amount of my life which isn't actually mentioned in the nasty things which I can remember, a whole side of my personality which sometimes I do not wish to acknowledge even to myself – or God. In the presence of the priest, however, I can be vulnerable enough to let all of it out, or at least what I know of it. The priest cannot turn away; he cannot introduce another subject of conversation or say, 'Another pot of tea, perhaps?' The confessor is there, sharing your wounds. The priest is the representative of the wounded and risen Christ. So when we go to confession, in whatever form it is done, the confessor allows us the freedom of the Kingdom to accept the fact that we are not as nice as we should be, or not as good as we could be. We are nothing like as holy as we are going to be. Acknowledging our sin we hear afresh the call to sanctity.

You do not prepare for confession by wondering about how things are going to be in the next world; you think about now, you think about your sin. This can usefully be done by reflecting on our failure to achieve virtue.

What are the virtues? They are faith, hope, love, prudence, fortitude, temperance, justice. As we think about the virtues we see ourselves through them as men and women in need of pardon and peace: the faithlessness that wasn't trusting in God; the hopelessness that hadn't attended to Christ's message that he is the Resurrection; the lovelessness that must have left the disciples in gloomy silence in that upper room. Faithlessness, hopelessness, lovelessness are all known to us in our own particular lives. Prudence? How stupid we are sometimes! Fortitude? What cowards! Temperance? What proppers-up of the bar! Justice? What a world we live in and represent – by those unfair and unkind comments which break the hearts of those who hear them and break our hearts too when we think about them afterwards. As we reflect on these virtues we know that we are in need of reconciliation and that we belong to a Church which preaches forgiveness – and not only preaches forgiveness but actually forgives, in God's name and with Christ's authority.

The Prayer Book Exhortation mentioned above recommends those who propose to receive Holy Communion 'to examine your lives and conversations by the rule of God's commandments'. Our predecessors in the faith knew the words of the Ten Commandments by heart and Anglicans heard them read at the beginning of the celebration of the Eucharist.

The wording of Exodus 20:1–17 together with the Lord's Prayer and the Apostles' Creed often appeared in decorated form above the altars of our churches and so they were readily available as a guide to conscience. The Christian today will still find his or her conscience prompted by reflecting on this fundamental passage in Holy Scripture as long as we are resolute in translating its meaning to the lives and circumstances of today. So seek it out and think it over.

In the contemporary Roman Catholic rite for the reconciliation of individual penitents, the person approaching the Sacrament of Reconciliation is advised to compare his or her life with 'the example and commandments of Christ'. Reflection on Mark 12:28–31, or its parallel in Matthew 22:34–40, will enable us to be prompted in conscience by the Holy Spirit.

> One of the scribes who had listened to them debating and had observed how well Jesus had answered them, now came up and put a question to him, 'Which is the first of all the commandments?' Jesus replied, 'This is the first: Listen, Israel, the Lord our God is the one Lord, and you must love the Lord your God with all your heart, with all your soul, with all your mind and with all your strength. The second is this: You must love your neighbour as yourself. There is no commandment greater than these.'

Arising from this, many people making their confessions sacramentally list their sins under three headings – sins against God, sins against others, and sins against self.

A vital reason for making going to confession a regular habit is that it makes us ready should that terrible moment occur when we commit the most awful thing we have ever done or fail drastically. In the familiar context of going to Father X or Mrs Y to make our confession we know that, although we have really sinned and let down God and ourself more completely than we ever thought possible, nevertheless we know exactly what to do – because the risen Lord is waiting at the confessional to offer us pardon and peace. Or, further, when that rather less terrible moment comes, when we are approaching a serious operation, or a very fresh and important stage of life, there is again the familiar means of grace, the risen Lord wanting to share our wounds with his and to evoke his joy and peace in our lives.

Many a Christian – and here's another reason for going regularly to confession – has grown as a man or a woman simply by hearing the perspectives of reason or love offered by the confessor after hearing our miserable list of twaddlesome nonsense and sadness. One of the burdens of sin is that it stops you from seeing clearly. After hearing your confession, priests won't say, 'Oh dear, dear, dear, why did you ever do that?' because they have done worse and know what the world is like, and they are in the position at that moment of hearing your holiness speaking with your sin: we make our confessions because grace is already moving in us. So priests offer private counsel and encouragement. We are taken seriously as saints in the making.

One final reason for going to confession regularly is that our sins compromise our proper fellowship with the Church and humankind. In a world full of injustice, wickedness, disunity, conflict and wrath, one of the purposes of the Sacrament of Reconciliation is to help build up churches as communities of men and women who are reconciled with Almighty God and with each other. It helps to make our fellowship closer and truer. It enables us to share the Body and Blood of the Lord at the Holy Table with greater joy.

In 1966, after our Archbishop Michael Ramsey came back from visiting Pope Paul VI, I heard him give a lecture on reunion. Archbishop Ramsey ended thus:

> I recall the scene in which the gift of the Divine Peace was actually made. Jesus came and stood among them. 'Peace be with you', he said, and showed them his hands and his side, and the wounds in his hands and his side are forever the cost of what that peace involves. And then he said, 'As the Father sent me so I send you. Whose sins ye remit, they are

remitted; whose sins ye retain, they are retained.' And is it not in the confessionals throughout Christendom that much of the work of Christian Unity is being done? Whenever a Christian kneels and confesses his sinfulness and hears the words of Christ 'Go in peace: your sins are forgiven' then the work of Unity is being done.

We want to be united in the Holy Spirit with ourselves, with our fellow Christians, with our fellow men and women, and with God and his Christ. It is in the Sacrament of Reconciliation that we can find one of the ways to do it. A Catholic's Rule of Life, therefore, will include a clear intention to go to confession on a regular basis – annually, or perhaps at Easter, Whitsun, in the Autumn and at Christmas – and to seek this means of grace at any time that he or she has fallen into grave sin. The three 'C's of Catholicism – Confession, Communion and Carry On – will take us to the grave and gate of death, and to the gate of heaven.

Giving

Although a Rule of Life is intended to help individual discipleship, no Christian lives properly without the Church. We are members one of another, parts of the Body of Christ, and a good deal of the happiness of being a Christian comes from participating in the Church's life. What we experience locally is an engagement with the one, holy, catholic and apostolic Church which we acknowledge in the Creeds. For this we often find ourselves profoundly thankful.

Part of our thanksgiving to God for life and the life of faith must be a stewardship of our money, time and talents. Thus we acknowledge God as the Giver of life and the Redeemer of it through Christ. This presents a challenge to us to devote a proper proportion of our time, abilities and money to the service of God's church. Earlier we had a brief glimpse of my mother before the 1920s with a silver threepenny bit in her glove for 'the collection'. Today loyal Anglican Catholics will recognise that they have to participate in funding the clergy, the church's buildings and its work. We do not just live on the endowments of the past! A Rule of Life therefore will include the assessment of what one intends to give directly to the local church. The decision on this should be approached not by working out what the proportionate contribution of one person should be, but by asking oneself what proportion of one's own income one should give.

Living under the Old Covenant the chosen people paid

'tithes' or 'tenths' of their annual possessions or money to pay the clergy, support the Temple worship and relieve the poor. Today there is no Church law to tell us what we must do. A recognised guideline, however, is to allot five per cent of our taxed income to our giving plus the returned income tax which Government will pass on to those with whom we make a covenant agreement. To make a commitment of this sort is to acknowledge our responsibility to God for the use we make of what we receive from his creation. Much of what we receive of course we must use simply for living – housing, feeding and caring for our dependants, and fulfilling our obligations to the State and the local community. These things are not to be neglected, nor the reasonable expectations of pleasure and recreation. 'Church', however, gives us so much and we should give in return.

Men and women who are unwaged or on low incomes will not be able to arrange for the Inland Revenue to return tax under a covenant! As members of the Body of Christ, however, they have exactly the same challenge to decide what they should give and then endeavour to respond.

Christian stewardship is not only about money, of course. It asks us to think of what we can offer to the life of the Church – but the scope of that lies outside the terms of a Rule of Life.

In St Matthew's Gospel at one point Jesus sends out the Twelve with the instruction, 'You received without charge, give without charge'. Can we apply this to ourselves in the succinct phraseology of the Authorised Version: 'Freely ye have received, freely give' (Matthew 10:8)?

Guidance

In these days of Cool Britannia 'everyone' – I learn from a glossy while waiting to have my hair cut – 'has their own personal trainer'! I am not sure about the grammar but this statement is a considerable exaggeration. As most of us stay away from training grounds, pools and gyms, most people are likely not to have personal trainers, except in the sense of shoes. Who can afford it, anyway?

Of course we do recognise that a coach or training partner can be a great help in sports or the pursuit of fitness. For the Christian man or woman – fit or unfit – it is also true that growth in Catholic faith and life can be encouraged by the help of another. Fr Kenneth Leech's splendid phrase for such a person is 'soul-friend'.

As you shape your Rule of Life, reviewing it and modifying it with experience, it should include the name of a man or woman, ordained or lay, whom you regard as someone you can call upon to help you sort out questions about yourself and your belief and practice. This choice requires some thought: those who suit some will not suit others. It could be your parish priest or your confessor. It could, however, well better be some other wise person, ordained or lay, known to you in the diocese or locally, perhaps someone recommended by a friend. You could ask for an initial, exploratory interview on the understanding that both would be looking to see if it would be good to proceed further.

At first it might then be a matter of a quarterly

consultation as the two of you get to know the matters that concern you. Later some people would continue to rely on a pattern of regular talks, but for others simply knowing that you can ring up and arrange a consultation when it is needed would be sufficient. There is a strength in the life of faith that comes from knowing that there is someone to whom you can go for guidance.

'The guidance game' is a phrase of Fr Martin Thornton. He uses it to describe what is usually called 'spiritual direction' and it is a useful term because it lacks some of the undertones of the more familiar title. In the guidance game we are trying to act on answering the question, 'What can one person do for another seeking fulfilment of God's particular purposes in life?' Martin Thornton stresses the unique character of the relationship between director and client. By 'client' I mean a Christian man or woman who on a regular basis consults someone else about the Christian life in its many aspects. By 'director' I mean another Christian who makes himself or herself available for the purpose. These two engage in the guidance game!

The term 'guidance game' clarifies the mental stance appropriate to the priest or deacon or layperson and client working together. It is not just a matter of the enlightened guiding the spiritually blind, or the knowledgeable teaching the ignorant, or the fit caring for the sick. Receiving direction should be thought of as coaching. The director is 'beside' the client, helping to look for the best in the individual and to bring it out, as both engage in a pilgrimage of discovery. The 'game' language suggests training and companionship, but also zest and enjoyment in the pursuit of God's providence. It also assumes tiredness, boredom, and the varying levels of achievement in people and between people in the pursuit of the Christian life. And in this pursuit the director is a coach.

What do coaches do? They watch and assess and suggest. They may not play superbly themselves, but they have knowledge and experience. They can challenge to produce special effort but in looking after training programmes they provide support at sticking points and sympathy in failure and despondency. The coach is interested in the player's potential and in bringing it out.

You may feel that all this sporty language is all very well, but what place has it got in Christian revelation? Have a look at 1 Corinthians 9:24–7:

> All the runners at the stadium are trying to win, but only one of them gets the prize. You must run in the same way, meaning to win. All the fighters at the games go into strict training; they do this just to win a wreath that will wither away, but we do it for a wreath that will never wither. That is how I run, intent on winning; that is how I fight, not beating the air. I treat my body hard and make it obey me, for, having been an announcer myself, I should not want to be disqualified.

Here St Paul is inviting us to take our individual Christian commitment in the Church very seriously – with the seriousness of the dedicated runner or the boxer. The Apostle's language is the language of enthusiasm for the game – and life is more than that! (I dare to write that during the World Cup.)

In the guidance game the first task of the coach or director is to listen. If the director is going to help another on the Christian pilgrimage there must be a high degree of respectful attention to what the client has to say – about believing, praying, living daily life. The second task is to help the client see possibilities of action in life – inward or outward – and to offer perspectives of Christian thought about them. He or she may just have to talk common sense or remind you of Christian doctrine. But it is not simply a matter of common sense or doctrine since coaching implies seeking how exactly they apply to the particular person who is seeking aid in following God's will better and clearer.

The guidance game does not mean 'guiding my client so that he is just like me, prays as I do or enjoys what I enjoy'. Obviously directors will have convictions that they will believe are normative for all Christians living the Catholic life, but outside the general rule of faith the director is not seeking conformity to particular styles or practices. Your director needs to know Holy Scripture and the Church's tradition in its breadth – not in the narrow sense of tradition with which we often meet today, where the attitudes of a faction in the last thirty years can parade under that great name – and this knowledge might be hoped for in a priest, a deacon, or a religious, but there is no reason at all for confining direction there. Lay direction is increasing. The aptitude and the attitude are all.

The director is not aiming at producing clones: as a coach he or she encourages personal freedom in the Spirit and in the context of the Church's faith and order. It is not that the director always comes up with good ideas. Sometimes in the client it is a case of 'Thank God, at least you give me a chance to speak'. And that can mean the relief of discovering what one had been trying to say. Because the director is 'there' the client can trust, utter and thus gain insight.

Some Christians are by religious instinct against the guidance game. To them it sounds like priestcraft in the bad sense of that word! The Spirit's life within us should do his own work. But the Spirit of God released into the world is a spirit of fellowship which creates the Church as Body of Christ, and the mutual concern of the director–client, coach–Christian relationship stirs that life into new forms and endeavours. The director cannot live your life for you or be your conscience. The Spirit of Christ within does that, subject to our human frailties, limitation and sin. As being a Christian means being a pilgrim and a seeker, the director as Christian friend and coach helps to clarify the way. He can suggest a retreat, he can suggest why things are boring or unrewarding which one time were not. The director helps you to kick about ideas – the guidance game again! – but it is you who sense – perhaps later – the direction actually to take.

Thus the guidance game is a true ministry of the Word. The director under God helps the client to hear it. At the same time because the game is in the Holy Spirit, over and over again it is the guide who all unbeknown is rebuked, instructed and inspired.

Questions

Worship

1. Why is the Eucharist the supreme act of Christian worship? How is this importance expressed in the ordering of the Sunday mass in which you participate? Reflect on the implications of the various names for the Eucharist.
2. Think about the weekend. What place does Sunday worship have in your life? Is it important or negotiable? How do you make choices for weekend activities? Do you see Sunday mass as an obligation to God and your fellow Christians?
3. What preparation do you make for Sunday mass? If necessary, what could you do to develop it?
4. What opportunities for contact with your fellow Christians does Sunday give you? What other opportunities do you have and how important are they to you?
5. You may go to church with spouse, partner or family or alone. Do you ever invite others as a matter of evangelism to accompany you? Consider how you might approach this.

Private Prayer

1. What is prayer for?
2. Review your prayer times on a daily and weekly basis. To what extent do you raise mind and heart to God as you go about your day? Consider how you might improve this. What symbols of faith are there in your home – apart from yourself, of course! Is there a crucifix, mini-crib at Christmas, picture of Jesus or Mary?

Where do you say your prayers?

3. Which of the four parts of prayer attracts you most and which do you find easiest? Reflect on the place that each one of them has in your prayer.
4. Check or make your own intercession list – people and causes. Reflect on your own beliefs about prayer for others.
5. Go through the order used for mass at your church. Can you identify the four parts of prayer in it?
6. Take opportunities to be silent with God in a quiet place or in church, perhaps kneeling before the reserved sacrament or a crucifix. Ask the Holy Spirit in whose life you share through baptism and confirmation, to focus your attention on Our Lord. Reflect on how you make your thanksgiving after Holy Communion.
7. What difference does posture make – kneeling, standing, sitting? Think about the use and meaning of the sign of the cross.
8. Check or make your own plan for private prayer.

Bible Reading

1. Catholic faith and life is founded on Scripture, tradition and reason. What place does the Bible have in your life? Think about what it means to say that the Bible is inspired.
2. What are your favourite parts of the Bible and why do you like them?
3. Do you think that all the parts of Holy Scripture are of equal value? Should we persist in trying to read books of the Bible which we find 'unrewarding'? Do you know what the readings will be at church on Sunday and do you look at them at home beforehand?
4. Check or make your own plan for regular Bible reading.

Holiness

Reconciliation

1. What does the term 'sins' mean to you. Do you think that people should be concerned about them? Is God concerned? When we say that Jesus is the Lamb of God who takes away the sins of the world, what does it mean?
2. How important to you is trying to live a Christ-like life? Do you think that holiness is possible for people today? If so, how?
3. Think about the place that penitence should have in the Christian life. What part should the Sacrament of Reconciliation have in it, generally and for yourself?
4. Who would you approach to discuss confession?
5. Are you a Catholic if you don't 'go to confession'?
6. Think and pray about the call to holiness. Then check or make your plan for regular confession.

Giving

1. What is the difference between charitable giving to good causes and contributing financially to your church? Do you believe that you have any obligations in these matters?
2. Have you any idea how much you spend on 'flag days' and the like, national appeals and beggars? How do you decide on the amount of giving to your church? Is 5 per cent of your taxed income a helpful figure? //
3. What opportunities for service are there in your church or your local community? Reflect on how you might offer yourself. What time or gifts do you have?
4. Sometimes people have gifts, interests or experience that they would like to use more fully or share with others. If this is the case with you, how do you think your church membership could help you to realise such hopes?
5. Check or make your own plan for the giving of money, time and talents.

Guidance

1. Reflect on the ways in which your own commitment as a Christian would be helped by personal guidance or consultation.
2. List some queries you have about the faith – in general or for yourself. With whom would it be useful to discuss them?
3. Thinking about the past, can you perceive ways in which God's work in your life has been forwarded or prompted by others? Have you found guidance from preaching, chats or discussion with your parish priest, reading, TV programmes? Is there any new direction which you might like to take now?
4. Reflecting on guidance, what appeals to you most: direction, coaching, a soul-friend, a teacher-pupil relationship, a hearing ear? If you are aware of need in this area, check or make your own plan for personal guidance.

A final question!

Check or make your own Rule of Life . . .